How Maui found his Mother

Peter Gossage

THIS IS THE story of Maui-tiki-tiki-a-Taranga, which means 'Maui formed in the topknot of Taranga'.

MAUI'S MOTHER, THE goddess Taranga, bore him prematurely and thought him still-born.

She cut the topknot from her head and tenderly wrapped his body in the long hank of thick, black hair.

TARANGA TOOK THE little bundle to the seashore. Calling upon Tangaroa, the God of the Sea, to take her son, she cast him into the ocean.

But Maui was still alive!

The wave children of Tangaroa and Hine-moana bore him on their backs.

The clouds shielded him from the fierce sun, and Tawhiri the wind cooled him.

The swelling tide swept him swiftly along the coast.

MAUI BOBBED ON the coastal waters for many days.

At last a friendly current drew him towards a seaside kainga nesting below a pa-topped bluff.

THE MOMENT THE topknot rolled ashore, fierce gulls, buzzing flies and stinging jellyfish fell hungrily upon it!

LUCKILY FOR MAUI, his uncle, Tama-nui-ki-te-Rangi, raced along the beach, scattered the predators, and carefully unwrapped the baby boy. He did not know that Maui was his nephew, but something in his heart made Tama take the child home to raise as his own son.

AS MAUI GREW, Tama taught him many things — of Rangi and Papa, Tiki and Tu.

He imparted to Maui the art of oratory and the tongue of a taiaha.

He told him of nature and aroha, and revealed to him the magic ways of mastering them.

MAUI LEARNT QUICKLY and was soon adept at changing his shape to that of any bird in the forest.
His favourite was Rupe, the wood pigeon.
One day he took this form and flew down to the kainga, where the men of the tribe were lazily digging the kumara patch.

MAUI SETTLED ON A KO.

Then he sang a chant of work. The men dug strongly to the beat of the song, and the job was quickly finished.

MAUI ENJOYED HIS childhood, but as he grew older one thing began to bother him.

All the other children in the pa had mothers.

Where was his?

'WHO IS MY mother?' he asked Tama.

'I think she is the goddess Taranga.'

'Where is she?'

'Far, far away, Maui. Too far for my old bones to take you,' said Tama.

'Then I shall go and find her myself,' determined Maui.

AND HE DID.

After many months and many miles of searching, Maui at last found the pa he had left so long ago.

There was a gathering in the pa, and as Maui crept closer he saw a woman greeting her sons.

He was sure that the woman was his mother.

ONE BY ONE, the woman gave her sons the hongi of greeting.

Maui silently entered the pa and stood behind the four brothers he had never met.

When Maui's turn came Taranga cried out, 'E! Who are you?'

'I am Maui-potiki, your last-born,' he answered, and he told his mother what had happened since she had cast him into the sea.

TARANGA'S EYES FILLED with happy tears.
She knew that this young man before her was indeed her son.
Maui-tiki-tiki-a-Taranga was happy too.
For he had found his mother.

The Maori words and their meanings

AROHA	love
HINE-MOANA	Goddess of the Sea
HONGI	the pressing of noses in a greeting
KAINGA	unfortified village
KO	wooden digging stick
KUMARA	sweet potato
PA	fortified village
PAPA	The Earth Mother
POTIKI	last-born
RANGI	The Sky Father
RUPE	wood pigeon
TAIAHA	long, hardwood weapon with a pointed tongue and a narrow blade
TANGAROA	God of the Sea
TAWHIRI	God of the Wind
TIKI	the first man, or pendant
TU	God of War